The Gr

Chat-Up Lines
and
Put Downs

Stewart Ferris

summersdale

THE WORLD'S GREATEST CHAT-UP LINES AND PUT DOWNS

Summersdale Publishers Ltd

46 West Street

Chichester

PO19 1RP

UK

www.summersdale.com

Printed and bound in Great Britain

ISBN 1 84024 470 4

The World's Greatest

Chat-Up Lines
and
Put Downs

What winks and shags like a tiger?

I don't know.

(Wink)

**I'd love to bury my head
in your cleavage.**

Just bury your head.

**I can read you like a book.
You're bound to be great
between the covers.**

*Well, you're not coming
anywhere near my spine.*

Shall we go all the way?

*Yes, as long as it's in
different directions.*

**If I were to ask you out,
would you accept?**

Accept what – defeat?

Will you have my children?

Sure!

**That's great – my babysitter's
just cancelled.**

When can I call you?

How about Saturday? I'm going away for the weekend.

I'd love to get into your knickers.

There's already one arsehole in there, and that's plenty, thank you.

Where have you been all my life?

I wasn't even born for the first half of it.

8

Let's be honest, we've both come here for the same reason.

You're right. I wanted to meet someone attractive and interesting. Would you excuse me?

**When I'm with you I feel
like a real man.**

So do I.

Do you sleep on your stomach?

No.

Can I, then?

**I've got a condom with
your name on it.**

*I doubt it, my name's not
Durex Extra Small.*

I'm sure I've noticed you before.

*And to think I hadn't even
noticed you at all!*

Wow.

Yuck.

**[Call her over using your finger]
I made you come using just one
finger. Imagine what I could
do with my whole hand!**

*Can you make yourself come
with just one finger?*

11

I'm trying to break the world record for snogging the most beautiful women in one evening. Care to be a part of history?

Sure, and since you'll be worth double points, it'll help me win my mates' dare to kiss as many ugly men as possible.

Can I have your number?

You'll find it in the phone book.

Aren't you going to tell me your name?

Don't worry, that's in the phone book too.

Come back to mine for a Bacardi and grope.

No thanks, I'll just have a gin and platonic.

When I was a prisoner of war they tortured me on the rack, and it wasn't just my legs they stretched...

What else, then – your imagination?

Have you ever experienced puppy love?

No, only monkey-spanking.

Would you like to come to bed with me? I've got an electric blanket...

Come home with me instead, I've got an electric chair.

14

I want to be served by the most attractive waitress. You do work here, don't you?

No, I just serve pizzas for fun.

You take my breath away.

I'd like to, and yet you carry on breathing.

God must have cried when you left heaven.

Yes, and he held a huge party when you left.

You and I would look sweet together on a wedding cake.

Only once you'd been cut in half.

Can I look up your skirt?

OK, if you can find the catalogue.

I'd like to run my fingers through your hair.

No thanks – I don't know where they've been.

When I look at you,
I know I've caught
the love bug.

*I'm so glad I was
inoculated.*

I've been waiting for you all my life.

Then you can wait a bit longer, can't you?

You bring me out in a hot sweat.

You bring me out in an allergic rash.

I could get lost in your eyes.

Why don't you just get lost?

Will you come out with me?

Out of the closet, definitely – meeting you makes me realise I'm no longer attracted to the opposite sex.

What's it like being the most attractive person here?

You'll never know.

You make my heart skip a beat.

How disappointing, I was aiming for a cardiac arrest.

**I don't expect to have sex
with you on our first date.
I'm quite restrained.**

*So am I, I don't even expect to
have a first date with you.*

**If you go out with me I'll
treat you even better than
I treat my sports car.**

*What, a good servicing every
10,000 miles or every ten months,
whichever comes first?*

**Weren't you on the cover of
Cosmopolitan recently?**

*Yes, and weren't you on the
cover of My Dog Weekly?*

Men like you remind me of holidays.

Holiday romance, you mean?

No, you're just never long enough.

Shall we go to your place or mine?

*Both. You go to yours
and I'll go to mine.*

**Has anyone ever told you
how beautiful you are?**

Yeah, loads of people.

**Can I help you out of
those wet clothes?**

*I don't think a wet blanket
would really help.*

I'm short of cash – could you buy me a drink?

I'm short of patience – no.

You're so sweet, you make my teeth ache.

You're so creepy, you make my skin crawl.

I'm a postman so you can rely on me to deliver a large package.

I need someone who comes more than once a day.

**I won't beat about your bush,
I've got something big that I'd
like to have between us.**

*That's what I thought
– the Atlantic Ocean.*

**I'd like to share with you
my passion for squash.**

I'm not thirsty.

**I'm really busy at the moment so
I can't ask you out, but why don't
we squeeze one in tonight?**

*I doubt it would be much of a
squeeze by the looks of you.*

Let me plug my laptop into your modem socket.

It's amazing how small they can make them these days.

I've just undressed you in my mind. You have a great body.

I did the same – you've got a nice personality though.

If I told you I have a big dick, would you shag me?

No.

Good, because it's actually very small.

Come and watch a sunset with me.

I'll pass, I've already seen one.

**I want to taste the salt of
the ocean on your lips.**

*You could always eat a bag of
Prawn Cocktail crisps instead.*

Can I wash your car for you?

Your hose wouldn't reach.

**Are you cold or are you hiding
Tic Tacs in your bra?**

*Are you cold or are you hiding a
Tic Tac in your underpants?*

27

**Come to a nudist beach with me
– I'll show you what I've got to offer.**

I've seen better in a packet of prawns.

**People think I'm a policeman
because of the size of
my love truncheon.**

*Yes, I remember Inch
High, Private Eye.*

**My yacht is stranded here for a few
days until the weather improves.
Want to keep me company on it?**

*That depends on the
size of your tender.*

I love you.

*I love chocolate,
but I'd never bother
chatting it up.*

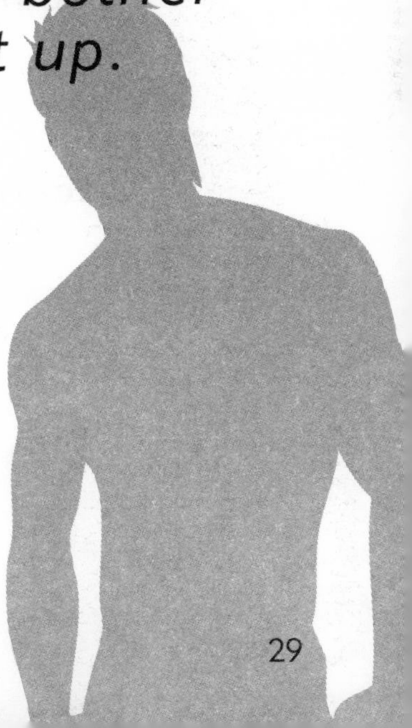

Would you like to come for a meal with me next week?

I would, but I just lost my appetite.

Nice legs. When do they open?

Nice mouth. When does it shut?

You're irresistible.

And you're completely resistible.

Would you like to come to a hilltop with me next week to watch the return of a comet that hasn't been visible for the last thousand years?

I've seen it.

I think we should leave together for the sake of the other women... you're making them look ugly.

I'm afraid not. You're making the other men look good.

There's something on your face, I think it's beauty. Let me try and get it off... oh, it's not coming off.

What a coincidence – neither are my clothes!

Your place or mine?

His.

You make me melt like ice cream, you make me boil like a kettle, and you make me gurgle like the morning after a curry.

You need medical attention.

Are you free tomorrow night?

No, but I'm on special offer the day after.

Your best feature would have to be my arms.

I would offer to shag your brains out, but someone's clearly beaten me to it.

I bet you a drink that you won't kiss me.

You win. Would you like the drink over your head?

You're cute.

My cute what?

Do you believe in love at first sight, or should I walk past you again?

I'd get myself some comfortable walking boots if I were you.

Shall I open the door for you?

*I'd rather you opened the
door for yourself.*

Let's spend the night together.

Sorry, I gave up babysitting years ago.

**I think the sun shines
out of your arse.**

*Well, you're living proof that
even a turd can be polished.*

I'm learning to be an artist and I'd like to paint you.

What colour?

If I kissed you I'd go weak at the knees.

That's because I'd give you a good kicking.

You're very attractive, but if you were any more vacuous your head would implode.

If you were a little bit more intelligent you'd be stupid.

Why don't we introduce ourselves?

Good idea – I'm going to introduce myself to that tasty bloke over there.

You look hot, can I take your temperature using my special thermometer?

I always bite thermometers.

What would you say to a little f**k?

Leave me alone, little f**k.

We could make beautiful music together.

I think I'll fetch my earplugs, actually.

Can I take you to meet my family?

OK, when are the visiting hours?

Is that a gun in your pocket or are you just pleased to see me?

It's a gun.

I'd like to take you out to eat.

Won't you eat me indoors?

**What would it take to get
a little kiss from you?**

Chloroform.

I want to fk you over
and over again.**

I want to f**k you over.

**Sorry if I'm dribbling, but I
had to get drunk before I could
come over and talk to you.**

*I wonder why pigs don't turn
into men when they drink...*

40

I'm a meteorologist, and I'd like to study your warm front. Let's go to an isobar and have a drink.

No thanks – I've seen the forecast. Damp in parts, hot and sticky with rising cumulonimbus. I'd rather stay at home.

I'm a musician. I'm famous for what I can do with my little piccolo.

That's nice. Did you say you were a musician as well?

You'd probably regret it in the morning if we slept together. So how about we sleep together in the afternoon?

Your approach wasn't bad, but I'd rather see your departure.

Why not be original and say yes?

No.

Don't you think that a man's charisma is more important than the size of his penis?

But you've haven't got any charisma either.

Shall we go and see a film?

I've seen it.

Excuse me, were you looking at me just then?

Yes, I thought from a distance you were good looking – I must stop leaving my glasses at home.

43

What's your name?

It begins with 'Mrs'. Shall I continue?

Can I be your love slave?

Well I certainly wouldn't pay you.

You really set me on fire.

Oh good, I was worried I didn't use enough petrol.

Would you like to go camping with me? Separate tents, of course.

That would be great, especially if we go to separate campsites too.

**Would you like a nibble
of my sausage?**

I think we should eat first.

Are you playing hard to get?

No, I'm playing impossible to get.

**I've got some condoms, so let's
sleep together right now.**

*Why, are they close to
their expiry date?*

Do you come here often?

Not if you do.

I could really turn you on.

It's no big deal. I can do it myself as long as I avoid thoughts of you.

Oi, darling, do you want to really enjoy yourself with me?

Sorry, I couldn't entertain the thought of spending time with someone who splits infinitives.

No, I'll pay for you as well.

You're utterly beautiful, but there must be something about you that's less than perfect. I expect you're a hopeless cook.

So nature's compensated you with perfect cooking abilities, then?

Would you like to come for a meal with me next week?

I'm on a diet.

What happened to your face? Do you step on rakes for a hobby?

No, I keep falling for you.

Go on, don't be shy, ask me out.

OK, get out.

Your face is familiar – I might even say commonplace.

Yours must be a limited edition, no one else would want one like it.

Did you know that men with the biggest dicks have the smallest mouths?

Your mouth needs its own postcode.

Mind if I take your picture?

As long as you bring it back.

Shall we go somewhere quieter?

*No need – I'll just put
on my earmuffs.*

Can I take you on a shopping trip?

*Wouldn't you rather just
take me in bed?*

May I have a drag on your fag?

*That's ironic – actually,
I am a fag in drag.*

**Will you hold my beer while
I go to the toilet?**

*Well it's preferable to what
you'll be holding.*

**I bet you've never done
it with a real man.**

Maybe not, but I bet you have.

**I like to think it's my vocation
to make women happy in bed.**

*Let me guess: you deliver meals
on wheels to the bed-bound?*

I like every muscle in my body. Especially yours.

What's a girl like you doing in a nice place like this?

**Do you know what would
look great on you?**

No.

Me.

**I'd like to demonstrate to you the
sexual equivalent of a marathon.**

*Go ahead. I'll just watch
from over there.*

**Most guys are like public toilets;
either vacant, engaged or full
of crap. Which are you?**

Er, could you repeat the question?

You make me drunk with passion, intoxicated with love and inebriated with desire.

It's got nothing to do with the ten pints you've drunk, then?

**On a scale of one to ten, you have been voted ten by everyone over there.
How do you feel?**

I use my fingertips.

Can I see your tits?

No, they've just migrated.

**I've had part of my body pierced.
Try and guess which bit.**

Your brain.?

Would you like my seat?

*I didn't realise transplant
surgery was so advanced.*

**Cheer up darling, it may
never happen.**

It just has.

I'm your cake. Would
you like to have
me or eat me?

*I'm not hungry, I
think I'll just give
you to the dog.*

Your face must turn a few heads.

And yours must turn a few stomachs.

What's your favourite record?

Sebastian Coe's 1,500 metres.

You know, being a millionaire can be pretty lonely without someone to share it all with.

I'll take a cheque.

What's your favourite film?

Kodak.

Which radio station would you like me to switch on in the morning?

Hospital radio.

I'm a helicopter pilot: fancy riding my chopper?

I'd rather just shag you.

**If you kiss me, I promise
not to turn into a frog.**

Why would I want to kiss you, then?

**When I was a prisoner of war,
held captive in a tower, the other
men used part of me to climb
down the wall and escape.**

Oh no, not you again?

**What would you say is
my best feature?**

Your ornamental pond.

When I look at the stars, I see your eyes. When I look at a flower I smell your perfume. When I look at the sun, I feel your warmth.

When I look at a cow, I see your bullshit.

I'm considering chucking my girlfriend for you.

Wow.

Are you impressed?

No, just surprised that you have a girlfriend.

Leaving already? Stay a minute and I'll get you a drink.

Just give me the cash – I'll save you the trouble.

Are you from Jamaica? Because Jamaican me crazy about you.

Nah, I'm from St Lucia. And I'm trying to lose ya.

What's the best way to get into your affections?

Via the North Pole.

I've circumnavigated the world single-handed.

What were you doing with your other hand, then?

Kiss me and I'll tell you a secret.

I know your secret – I work at the clinic.

Hello, I'm a stamp collector.

Well, you're not mounting me.

**You've got the best body
I've ever seen.**

*Thanks, I wish I could say
the same for you.*

**You could if you were as
big a liar as me.**

**Which part of my bed would
you like to sleep on?**

Is there a top bunk?

I never forget a face.

Neither do I usually, but in your case I'll try to make an exception.

**May I have the pleasure
of this dance?**

No, I'd like some pleasure too.

**How would you like your
eggs in the morning?**

Unfertilised, preferably.

How did you get to be so beautiful?

*When they were handing out the
good looks, I was given your share.*

**Would you like to come out with
me for some coq au vin?**

What sort of van do you drive?

Where can I find mutual love?

At the start of a tennis match.

**It's funny, I know I'm a bit drunk,
well, very drunk, but I'm sure
I know you from somewhere.
Any chance of a kiss?**

Go home, Dad.

**Will you come out with
me on Saturday?**

*Sorry, I'm having a really bad
headache at the weekend.*

You look like a model.

No, I'm real.

**I'd go to the end of the
world for you.**

*Thanks, but would you
stay there for me?*

You look like my wife.

How long have you been married?

I'm not married.

You've got a smile that could light up a whole town.

You've got a mouth that could accommodate a whole town.

You're so hot, you're melting the elastic in my underwear.

I wondered what the smell was.

Shall I tell you my name so we're ready for later?

What do you mean?

So you'll know what to scream.

Where is the toilet?

*Wow, I didn't realise you
were house trained.*

**I want people to love me for
myself, not for my money.**

*Isn't that narrowing your
options somewhat?*

This is my dog, Raffles.

Oh, isn't he big? Can I stroke him?

**Of course. Would you like to
stroke Raffles as well?**

71

Can I have a tinkle on your piano?

I'd rather you used the toilet.

The name's Thomas, John Thomas.

I'm Holly – I'm used to little pricks.

Please would you talk to me so that creep over there will leave me alone?

I just said that to someone about you.

What would you say if I asked you to marry me?

Nothing. I can't talk and laugh at the same time.

Let's skip the awkward beginning and pretend we have known each other for a while. So, how's your Mum?

She told me I wasn't to see you anymore.

Can you give me your name, please?

I don't think that it would suit you.

Every time I come here I've seen you. I'd like to know more about you.

So would the police.

74

I always swallow.

*Glad to hear it, you'd
starve otherwise.*

**People must tell you this all the
time, but you're very beautiful.**

*Well you're so ugly, Frankenstein's
monster would go to a
Hallowe'en party as you.*

Have you got any Irish in you?

No.

Would you like some?

Yes please, mine's a Guinness.

75

**How do you keep an
idiot in suspense?**

Don't know.

**Neither do I, I'm hoping
someone will tell me...**

Are you separated?

No, it's just the way I walk.

**I'm a photographer for a model
agency: I've been looking
for a face like yours.**

*I'm a plastic surgeon. I've been
looking for a face like yours.*

What sign were you born under?

'No entry'.

Will you call me pretty soon?

*No, you're not pretty now and
I doubt that'll ever change.*

Let me be really dirty with you.

You smell as if you already are.

Where do you come from?

Way above your league.

Are you as hot as me?

No, why don't you get some air to your brains by undoing your flies?

You've got such a heavenly body, I've named a star after you.

By the look of your body, someone should name a bouncy castle after you.

I can fulfil your sexual fantasy.

Where's your horse, then?

Excuse me, would you help me with an itch that I can't reach?

Just rub it against the lock on my chastity belt.

Hello, you don't know me, but I've just come back from the future in which you and I have the most passionate love affair. And it started tonight.

And I've just come back from even further in the future where I found out that we're brother and sister, so I think it's best that we change history.

You've got great boobs.

So have you.

I think of my body as a temple.

It looks more like an amusement park.

I think I could make you very happy.

What, leaving already?

Can I pinch your bum?

As long as I can I pinch your wallet.

Do you want to play my organ?

Only if it's got some good rhythms.

Fancy a champagne breakfast?

*How thoughtful, could you
get it delivered tomorrow?*

I'd like to marry you.

I'd rather skip straight to the divorce.

**You look like a horse and I'm a
hedge. Would you like to jump me?**

*I think pruning would
be a better idea.*

It's not how big it is, it's what you can do with it.

Well, making it invisible to the naked eye is obviously your special talent.

I thought paradise was further south?

It is, it's miles away.

You make me feel like a squirrel. I'd like to pile my nuts up against you.

You remind me of a rat, and the Pest Control department is on the way.

If you were a food, you'd be caviar. If you were a word, you'd be serendipity. If you were a car you'd be a Rolls Royce.

If you were a real man I might stay and talk to you.

**Would you like to see
something swell?**

*Yes, the bruise I'm about
to inflict on your face.*

That's a really nice dress.

*Thanks, but there's no way
you'll talk me out of it.*

**Would you like to come back to
mine? You can subtract your clothes,
divide your legs and we'll multiply.**

*How about you leave by the square
route? The back door's that way.*

I've got the body of a Chippendale.

Wow, where do you keep it?

If I asked you to have sex with me, would your answer be the same as the answer to this question?

I don't know what your problem is, but I bet it's hard to pronounce.

Do you receive mail often?

I do actually, and that does not count as a package.

Excuse me, do you have the time by any chance?

Do you have the energy?

[Touch his shirt] **Is this cotton?**

No.

[Indicate his crotch area] **Oh, but this must be felt...?**

So, do you have a job?

Yes, I'm a female impersonator.

Life's a bitch, mind if I throw you my bone?

If I throw a stick, will you leave?

I'm a really deep thinker.

Yes, you look lost in thought. That must be unfamiliar territory.

How about we have a baby together?

If I wanted to hear the pitter patter of tiny feet, I'd put shoes on my cat.

Stay still, I'm trying to pick you up.

Wait a second, I'm trying to imagine you with a personality.

You're gorgeous. Mind if I paint you and make you my Mona Lisa?

Just because no one understands you, it doesn't make you an artist.

90

**You're at the top of my list
of things to do today.**

*You look like you're at the top of
the country's 'most wanted' list.*

**Why don't we meet here
again sometime?**

*Um, where should I start? Your
bad breath, my boyfriend...*

**I'm single cream, whip
me up into a frenzy.**

I would, but it looks like a small trifle.

You look like you haven't changed your shirt in a fortnight.

That's impossible, I've only had it a week.

Look, to decide whether or not we should date, let's toss for it.

OK. Heads – you don't get to go out with me, tails – I don't get to go out with you. Fair?

What would you give me if I agreed to sleep with you?

Syphilis.

**We could have quite
a future together.**

*What a coincidence! I
think I have a future with
that man over there.*

If you should ever happen to fall in love with me, I'll be waiting for you.

If I ever get that desperate, I won't be worth waiting for.

Is your body real?

No, you have to inflate it through my mouth every ten minutes.

Hi, didn't we sleep together once?

Well I never make the same mistake twice.

Imagine we're in love.

OK, I'll try. Nope, it's just not working.

Are your legs tired? You've been running through my mind all evening.

I was looking for a brain cell.

You're so funny – you should be on television.

Really?

Yeah, then I could turn it off.

**Have you got a pickaxe
I could borrow?**

No, why?

I'd like to break the ice.

**Don't go away, I'm just about
to put the kettle on.**

Are you sure it's your colour?

May I introduce myself?

*Certainly – try those people over
there, they look desperate.*

Do you think you could fall for me?

Only if you pushed me.

Am I your dream come true?

*I don't know yet. Go and
stand in the road with your
eyes closed, and we'll see.*

**If I had known I was going to meet
someone as gorgeous as you tonight,
I'd have had my eyebrows plucked.**

*If I'd known I was going to meet
someone as ugly as you, I'd have
had my eyeballs plucked.*

**It must have been fate that
brought us together.**

No. It was just plain bad luck.

Where can we go from here?

I don't care, so long as you go first.

It's OK, we can be together tonight. I've given my girlfriend the evening off.

What for? Good behaviour?

I've lost my script, so we'll have to ad lib.

I don't think much of your part.

Do you mind if I smoke?

I don't care if you burn.

You seem like a sensible girl to me.

That's right – I'm not coming anywhere near you.

I just noticed you standing on your own, can I cheer you up?

OK, bye.

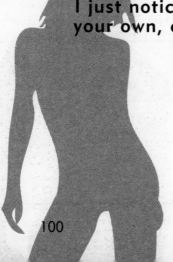

Do you kiss with your eyes closed?

I would if I was kissing you.

What would you say is the best thing about being so gorgeous?

Not being expected to talk to ugly sods like you.

It must be my birthday because the sight of you is the best gift possible.

No – what about your natural gift for repulsing women?

Would you like me to lick champagne out of your navel?

No, but you can lick the fluff out of it.

You've turned my floppy disk into a hard drive.

Sorry, I don't date men with tiny peripherals.

Bond. James Bond.

Off. Piss off.

Help me – I'm drowning in a sea of love!

Tough, I can't swim.

103

Hey, you're not much of a looker, but I'll have you.

Thanks, you must be very open-minded. Was that how your brain slipped out?

You don't sweat much for a fat girl.

I will when I start running away from you.

Hi. I'm a tenor.

Sorry, I've only got a fiver.

That outfit would look great in a crumpled heap on my bedroom floor.

That shirt would look great on someone slimmer.

The word of the day is 'legs'. How about we go back to my place and spread the word?

No, it's OK. I'm going to another party tonight, I'll spread it there.

Are you a criminal?

No.

But you're most wanted.

Didn't we used to be lovers?

Yes. I left you because you have an infuriating memory problem.

Your face is absolutely perfect.

So is yours... for radio.

**You've got everything a man could
want: teeth, hair, moustache...**

All I lack is your charm and subtlety.

**Where did you get those
big blue eyes?**

They came free with my face.

I haven't done this sort of thing before. Will you teach me?

OK, go out of that door, close it gently behind you, and go away.

Listen, I want to tell you something... I'm not wearing any underwear.

Don't worry – there's a sale on at Marks and Spencer's.

Hey, don't I know you?

Not yet. Ask me another.

Before I buy you a drink, can you tell me if you like me?

Get the drink first. We'll deal with the bad news later.

How about coming back to my place for a bit of heavy breathing?

Why, is the lift broken?

Where shall we go for our honeymoon?

What about Neverland?

Would you like to join me in a glass of wine?

There wouldn't be room for both of us.

How much do you charge?

I don't normally charge, but for you I'd make an exception.

Weren't you at that party last week?

Yes. And I haven't changed my mind since then, I'm afraid.

I would love to give myself to you.

Sorry, I'm afraid I don't accept bribes.

I'm very in touch with my inner self.

I bet your psychiatrist makes you lie face down on the couch.

It's very difficult to get served in here. What are you having in case I get served first?

An attack of nausea.

Kiss me.

You'll have to drug me first.

I've waited all my
life to meet you.

*And you couldn't think
of a good chat-up
line in all that time?*

Let's get together, you and me. You know you want to.

No thanks. I don't date outside of my species.

The trouble with this place is some of the people that come here.

Well do something about it then – leave.

Queuing is so boring, don't you find?

It is now.

**Nobody I know can tell me
who you are, I'm sure I've seen
you somewhere before...**

*Maybe. Take that ugly mask off so I
can see what you really look like.*

No, don't tell me – you're a Pisces?

OK, I won't tell you.

**Isn't it boring here? Do you
want to go somewhere else?**

*Why don't you? That should
liven things up a bit.*

I promise I'll go through anything for you.

Great. Let's start with your bank account.

Can I buy you a drink?

I would think so – why don't you ask the barman?

Um, hello.

Oscar Wilde, I presume?

Are you sisters?

Yes.

You must have left Cinderella at home.

Have you ever tried drinking Australian wine?

What else would I do with it?

I've seen your beautiful face before, I'm sure.

Yes, I'm friends with your wife.

You know what I like most about you? All of you.

Well, I'm an all or nothing sort of person, and with you it's nothing.

**Let me make you dinner
– I'm a great cook.**

No thanks, I'm not much of an eater.

Would you like another drink?

*I don't think our relationship
will last that long*

Do you know what I am?

A eunuch?

**You have the bluest eyes
I've ever seen.**

*Thanks. I had them re-
sprayed just yesterday.*

**Would you like to wear
real animal fur?**

*I'd wear rat fur if it provided an
extra layer between me and you.*

**Would you like to go to
bed with me tonight?**

*I'm afraid I can't – I haven't
anything to wear.*

120

I want people to like
me for who I am.

*Is that why you
drive a Porsche?*

If love is a drug, I'm addicted to you.

As for me, I just say no.

**Women say I have the
gift of the gab.**

Wrap it up, then.

Can I count on your vote?

Are you sure you can even count?

Do you know the difference between fellatio and focusing?

No.

Would you mind helping me adjust my telephoto lens, then?

You look good enough to eat.

Shame you need to diet, then.

You're hot. You should feel guilty for causing global warming.

Well, I'm not coming anywhere near you from the smell of those natural gases.

This time next year, we'll be laughing together about this.

I'm already laughing.

Would you like a raisin?

No.

OK. How about a date?

I'm afraid I have to arrest you. You have been trespassing in my mind and you stole my heart.

At least, unlike you, I haven't been robbed of my dignity.

Can I give you an Australian kiss? It's like a French kiss, but down-under.

No, just go home and away from here.

You're just my type: gorgeous smile, great body, amazing personality. It's just a shame about your clothes.

What about them?

You're still wearing them.

Kiss me quick.

Fuck me slowly.

I'd like to make love to you.

Let's just skip to the post-coital fag.

The doctor said I should release my fluids regularly. Would you mind if I used your body?

I'll lend you a cup.

Hey, don't go yet... You've forgotten something.

What?

Me.

Excuse me, I'm new around here. Can you give me directions to your bedroom?

I'm not very good with directions, you'd better ask my boyfriend.

Can you tell me the time, because I want to make a note of the moment we first met.

I'll give it to you twice, because it's also the time we split up

I know a great way to burn off the calories from that sandwich.

Yes, it involves running away from you.

Excuse me, aren't we related?

No, and I'd like to keep it that way.

You look like you've
never done it in
a waterbed.

*You look like you've
never done it in a bed.*

Is your dad a thief?

No.

Then how did he steal the stars out of the sky and put them in your eyes?

Is your dad a thief?

Yes.

Can he get me a DVD player?

'Yes' is my favourite word. Is it yours?

No.

I've got a couple of tickets to the theatre on Saturday.

Great – I've got a friend I can invite, unlike you.

Congratulations! You've won first prize in a competition: a date with me!

Oh. What was second prize? Two dates with you?

Am I the light of your life?

No, you're far too dim.

If you were a building, you would
be the Palace of Versailles.

And you'd be a pig barn.

Do you believe in magic?

*Yes, I'm always making men
like you disappear.*

I have designs on you.

*You had better go back to
the drawing board.*

If I could see you naked, I'd die happy.

If I could see you naked, I'd die laughing.

I'm like quick-drying cement: after I've been laid, it never takes me long to get hard.

And then can I walk all over you?

Would you go crazy if I went out with you for a couple of months and then left you?

I'd go crazy if you went out with me for a couple of months and didn't leave.

I've always been fascinated by beautiful women. Mind if I study you?

Let's make it a joint project: I've always been fascinated by ugly men.

I'm here! So, what exactly were your two other wishes?

To meet a handsome guy and live in Barbados; you must be the man from the lottery.

Can I stand here and flirt with you?

I'll get you a chair. People might think you're my mother.

You're just my type.

That's right – female!

I'd like to take you to dinner.

*Sure – can you pick me
up afterwards too?*

Are you happy?

I was.

**What do you think of
the music here?**

Better than the company.

What's the biggest problem in your life?

Look in a mirror.

My friends told me all about you.

What friends?

You've got a face like a peach.

And you've a face like a prune.

**I'm Mr Right – someone said
you were looking for me.**

I think it's a case of mistaken identity.

Can I tickle your belly?

Only if you can do it from the inside.

What's the difference between a game of poker and some hot sex?

I don't know.

Fancy a game then?

I climb mountains for a hobby, but getting on top of you is going to be my biggest challenge.

That depends on the length of your rope.

**I recognise you from somewhere
– didn't we go to school together?**

No. I was your maths teacher.

**[Gesture towards his trousers]
Hey, is that a mirror I can
see in your pocket?**

No, why?

**Because I'm sure I can see
myself in your trousers.**

**I'm going to follow you home,
so will you keep me?**

I'd only put you down.

Do you come here often?

No, I usually do it in bed.

I never like to come second, but I'll make an exception in your case.

I don't usually turn down men like you – but I'll make an exception in your case.

When I roll across my satin sheets at night, the sound reminds me of you.

What, while I'm eating a packet of crisps?

My stars said I would meet the woman of my dreams tonight.

I'll go and see if I can find her for you.

Can I kiss you?

Of course, but mind you don't burn yourself on my cigarette.

I'm sure I could turn you on.

You couldn't even turn on a radio.

Nice shoes. Will you sleep with me?

Nice brain, shame batteries aren't included.

**I've been looking for
you for a lifetime.**

*I've already had enough of
you to last a lifetime.*

**Aren't you famous? You're
much taller in real life.**

Yes, I am. It's a shame that The
World's Best Transvestite *is the
only thing I've starred in.*

Haven't we just slept together?

No.

**Oh not again... my watch
is an hour fast.**

144

I've got two words for you: 'you' and 'me'.

That's three words, and they don't go together very well.

**Meet me around the back
in two minutes?**

Whose back?

**I'm bored of stunning women, I
think I need someone like you.**

*That's OK then, because I think
stunning women is illegal.*

What's your sign?

*Let me guess yours – it's the
first sign of madness.*

I'd die for you.

Good – crawl off and die then.

Have you ever been abroad?

No, I've always been a bloke.

**I'm sorry, were you trying
to get my attention?**

No.

Amazing, you didn't even have to try.

147

**How long until you call
me 'boyfriend'?**

I don't want to call your boyfriend.

Are you a fish?

No.

**But you're definitely
catch of the day.**

Your plaice or mine?

**Do you like swimming? Can I
show you my breaststroke?**

*No thanks, tuck your shirt in, I'm not
enjoying watching your belly flop.*

Can I buy your love?

There's no way you could afford it.

I write poetry, will you be my muse?

You don't need me. You're amusing enough as you are.

Get your coat, you've pulled.

Push off.

You're like a good wine, you improve with age.

You're like a good cheese, you smell awful.

150

With you, I can really feel myself.

We'd all prefer you did that in private.

**You'll never find anyone
like me again.**

Well, that's a cheering thought.

**Hey baby, let's do it
with the light on.**

Shut up and close the car door.

The Little Book of Flirting

Stewart Ferris

£2.99 Pb

Welcome to the definitive guide to flirting in the 21st century. Learn essential tips such as how to make your first impression count, when physical contact works (and when it doesn't), what to say and, more importantly, when to leave them guessing. Actions speak louder than words and in the universal language of flirting this book is the essential phrasebook.

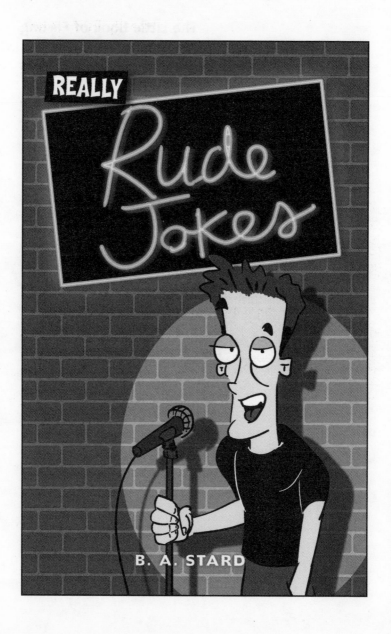

Really Rude Jokes

B. A. Stard

£4.99 Pb

The crudest classrooms, the sleaziest bars and the smuttiest office e-mails have been dredged for this bumper collection of dirty jokes – so fucking funny you'll piss yourself.

Raunchily rude and sensationally lewd, *Really Rude Jokes* is the ultimate bad influence for all gutter-dwelling minds.

Really Daft Ideas

D. I. Saster

£4.99 Pb

Some ideas should never have made it further than the half-witted minds they originated from. *Really Daft Ideas* picks out the pottiest true stories to make you laugh and cringe.

From the soldier who tied a hammock between two wall lockers, only to be fatally crushed by them at bedtime, to the man who took aim at a spider crawling up his leg and shot himself instead, this book demonstrates why it's a good idea to think before you act.

ADVANCED SWEARING HANDBOOK

MARK LEIGH & MIKE LEPINE

Advanced Swearing Handbook

Mark Leigh & Mike Lepine

£4.99 Pb

Uncut, uncensored and totally outrageous, this guide to profanity old and new includes the most offensive song titles, the nastiest names for private parts, and the most unfortunate place names from Arsoli to Wetwang. Prepare to be amazed, shocked and highly amused, as the unapologetic Kings of Cussing show that swearing can be very funny indeed.

Mike Lepine and **Mark Leigh** have collaborated on numerous TV comedy and trivia-based shows and have written more than 30 humorous books together including *How to be a Real Man* (with Julian Clary), *The Politically Incorrect Handbook*, *How to be a Complete Bastard* (so obscene that questions were asked in the House of Commons), *How to be a Complete Bitch*, *The Really Rude Holiday Guide* and *You Know You're a Child of the '80s When...*